Will's Pet

by Myka-Lynne Sokoloff

illustrated by Adam Record

"Can I have a pet?" asked Will.

Mom said, "Yes, you can. What kind of pet would you like?"

Will thought about it.
"I would like a giraffe!"
he said.

Mom laughed.
"A giraffe will not fit in
a bed!"

"How about a hippo?"
Will said.

Dad said, "A hippo will hog
all the room in the tub!"

"How about a porcupine?"
asked Will.

Mom smiled.
"You can't pet a porcupine!"

Will asked, "Can I get
a pig?"

Dad said, "Oh no, a pig will
eat too much!"

Dad and mom shook
their heads.
"No giraffe,
no hippo,
no porcupine,
no pig."

Will thought about it.

"What about — a dog?"
he asked.

Mom looked at Dad.
Dad looked at Mom.

"A dog? Great idea!"

Will said, "Dogs make the
best pets of all!"